# WILDERNESS

the taunt may turn out to contain a gift

# WILDERNESS TAUNTS

## REVEALING YOUR LIGHT

Ian Adams

**CANTERBURY**
**PRESS**
Norwich

© Ian Adams 2016

First published in 2016 by the Canterbury Press Norwich
Editorial office
3rd Floor, Invicta House
108–114 Golden Lane
London EC1Y 0TG, UK

Hymns Ancient & Modern® is a registered trademark
of Hymns Ancient and Modern Ltd

Canterbury Press is an imprint of Hymns Ancient & Modern Ltd
(a registered charity)
13A Hellesdon Park Road, Norwich,
Norfolk NR6 5DR, UK

www.canterburypress.co.uk

Text and photography by Ian Adams
The photograph on p. 1 features the artwork 'There will be no miracles'
by Nathan Coley in the grounds of the Scottish National Gallery of
Modern Art Two, Edinburgh
Photographs for Taunts 21 and 40 feature details of the
Barbican Mural Plymouth by Robert Lenkiewicz

British Library Cataloguing in Publication data

A catalogue record for this book is available
from the British Library

978 1 84825 917 1

Printed and bound in Great Britain by
Ashford Colour Press

may you rediscover the light of your hope

# CONTENTS

to be a hopeful human being in the 21st century
is a demanding task

© text and photography by Ian Adams

to better understand who we are
to reconcile with our shadows

# INTRODUCTION

To attempt to be a hopeful human being in the 21st century is a demanding thing. This book seeks to explore that task through a series of 40 meditations with photographic images. It draws on the Gospel accounts of the 40-day testing of Jesus in the wilderness. The temptations he faced there may be best understood as taunts seeking to throw him off balance. This book imagines what might be the taunts that we face now, whenever the light of our hope is confronted by the darkness in the world, and by the shadows within ourselves.

These meditations attempt to look beyond any obvious temptation urging us to do something wrong, and to recognize the deeper questions that are being asked of us about life, about love and about faith. If we are truly attentive, each taunt may turn out to contain a gift, enabling us to better understand who we are, to reconcile with our shadows, to discover the deeper truth of our light, and so to step with imagination and generosity into whatever is being called of us.

The meditations emerged initially from personal experience. The core of each reflection was written in real time in Lent 2015. I wanted to enter Lent without easy answers, and to open myself up to this most searching of seasons. Taking the taunts faced by Jesus as a beginning point, I re-imagined the taunts that might come my way. Around the twelfth day I began to regret having started out on this journey at all, such was the intensity of the struggle in which I found myself.

Fearful of where I was taking others – I was sharing the taunts that surfaced each day on Morning Bell[1] – I came close to abandoning the project. But I felt that the visceral reality of what I was experiencing indicated that something important was happening within me. I wanted to remain curious about whatever was throwing me off balance.

---

1  belovedlife.org/morning-bell

to discover the deeper truth of our light

Each meditation is an attempt to hear and receive the taunts that might surface for us without defensiveness, and then to respond with authenticity. These personal meditations are offered here in a hunch that they contain elements of our shared human condition. You may find something of yourself in this journey into the wilderness.

*Wilderness Taunts* emerged originally in the context of Lent, but our experiences of wilderness are rarely confined to any one season. The meditations can be followed through from 1 to 40. They can also be used on their own, or mixed and matched.

The book opens with the stunning Gospel accounts of the temptation of Jesus as told by Matthew and Mark. Each meditation is accompanied by a Prayer Word, a photographic image and a line from Psalm 88.

The Prayer Word is a short prayer or mantra that emerged from my attempt to work with each taunt. A guide to using the Prayer Word is included with other creative suggestions at the end of the book. The photographic images attempt to explore the sombre beauty – the wilderness – of our urban and coastal environments. Jesus would have known the Psalms well – probably by heart – and we can imagine him finding Psalm 88 to be a welcome precursor of his own wilderness experience, and a tough but comforting presence in a dark place.

This is a demanding book, as it should be. As the wilderness tested Jesus, so these Wilderness Taunts ask much of us. The taunts are tough, the images have a bleak quality, and the language is raw. The core of each meditation remains as it was originally experienced by the writer, reflected on and written up each day in Lent.

The wilderness is the place of deepest learning. In the toughness of the Wilderness Taunts may you rediscover the light of your hope for yourself, for your communities, and for the world – and may you know that in God's grace and love, all shall be truly well.

Wild beasts may come, but so too may angels ...

the sombre beauty – the wilderness –
of our urban and coastal environments

# FOETAL

I wake
at dawn
inside a dream
through which I fly, an eagle
in slow high circles
the cool clear space
between sleep and wakeful
and below
in deep snow
are the tracks of one who has wandered
stopped and stumbled,
a trail of lost or discarded things.

They lead to a man
naked and foetal, settled
for death. Or for birth.

I recognise this man.
He stirs.

these Wilderness Taunts ask much of us

# THE TAUNTING OF JESUS

**Matthew 4.1–11**

Then Jesus was led up by the Spirit into the wilderness to be tempted by the devil. He fasted for forty days and forty nights, and afterwards he was famished. The tempter came and said to him,
'If you are the Son of God,
command these stones to become loaves of bread.'
But he answered, 'It is written,
"One does not live by bread alone,
but by every word that comes from the mouth of God."'

Then the devil took him to the holy city and placed him on the pinnacle of the temple, saying to him,
'If you are the Son of God,
throw yourself down; for it is written,
"He will command his angels concerning you",
and "On their hands they will bear you up,
so that you will not dash your foot against a stone."'
Jesus said to him, 'Again it is written,
"Do not put the Lord your God to the test."'

Again, the devil took him to a very high mountain and showed him all the kingdoms of the world and their splendour; and he said to him, 'All these I will give you, if you will fall down and worship me.'
Jesus said to him, 'Away with you, Satan! for it is written,
"Worship the Lord your God,
and serve only him."'

Then the devil left him, and suddenly angels came and waited on him.

**Mark 1.12–13**

And the Spirit immediately drove him out into the wilderness. He was in the wilderness for forty days, tempted by Satan; and he was with the wild beasts; and the angels waited on him.

he was in the wilderness for forty days

# [01] WHO ARE YOU?

No really, who are you?
You have no idea.

You know that you are not the person you aspire to be.
And you are rarely how others think of you.
Who are you?

Some recognition that you do not know who you are
may be a very good place to begin this wilderness journey.
Let go of all your accumulated conceptions
and misconceptions
to clear the way for whatever may be true.

Knowing nothing is a humiliation.
It may also be a gift.

And perhaps, echoing a name from an old story
of how God describes God – I Am
– the gift may be a discovery that You Are.

And that You Are loved.
And that You Are love.

## PRAYER WORD

**I Am loved, I Am love**

O Lord, God of my salvation,
when, at night, I cry out in your presence

Psalm 88.1

# [02] YOU WILL BREAK

The possibility of you getting through 40 days
of testing is nil.
This is the desert.
Welcome, says the tempter, to my world.

And you know that you will break.
You will slowly disintegrate.
Or you will shatter.
In some brittle moment.
Or through the course of one too-long day,
just when you imagined you were going to emerge intact.
You will break, you know you will.
On your own, you will snap,
a dried stick in the undergrowth.
You will break.

But could it be that your breaking here may open up
the path to some deeper healing?
The breaking of your own capacity
to fix, to achieve and to succeed
may be an essential step on your path towards maturity.

So do not be alarmed when you hear something crack.
And may the breaking leave you tender.

## PRAYER WORD

**I break, become tender**

let my prayer come before you
Psalm 88.2

# [03] YOUR APPETITE WILL WIN

There is only one outcome.
You may try to disguise it, ignore it, deny it.
But it is true all the same.
Your appetite has power.
Your drug of choice.
Your appetite will win.


And yet you know, even as you hear it,
that this taunt reveals a glimpse into your true appetite.

Some deeper impulse has always been present.
Those longings for intimacy and for comfort, for bliss
and for at-oneness are signs of some greater desire.
Of your yearning for the Mystery,
for the Spirit,
for the Christ,
for the Father and Mother of all.

Nurture this desire.
And you will discover that their desire is for you.


## PRAYER WORD

**I yearn for you**

incline your ear to my cry
Psalm 88.2

# [04] YOU HAVE WASTED SO MUCH

How could you waste so much?
So many opportunities let pass.
So many poor decisions.
So few adventures embraced.
So few risks taken.
You have wasted so much.


Yes, there has been wastage.
And you cannot recover what is lost.
But still you are here,
with a sense of calling, some learning, much love,
and many friends.

So what is to be done?
You could hurry back towards whatever you missed.
Or cram in new achievements.

Resist both those courses of action.
Instead, vow to follow, with love
the path that opens up from here.
Resolve to make this season a time of attention
to the task before you.
And ponder the possibility that in God
nothing is wasted.


## PRAYER WORD

**in you, nothing wasted**

for my soul is full of troubles
Psalm 88.3

# [05] TURN AROUND. GO BACK

Turn back now.

You are right to fear what lies ahead
And turning back is the better option.
You have taken a path that ever narrows,
towards a destination that does not exist.
You know the sick feeling that the path you could have taken
has been lost to you.
Turn around.
Go back.


And yet.
If you can find the courage to stay on the path
new possibilities may reveal themselves.

There will be a way
– may you be guided –
out onto the wide open moor
that awaits you.
Into sunlight.
Keep on.


## PRAYER WORD

**I keep on, guide me**

and my life draws near to Sheol
Psalm 88.3

# [06] THERE IS AN EASIER ROAD

There still is time.
Look for another route.

It's only day 6 and you are regretting setting out on this path.
Everything is so relentless.
The tough path.
This arid desert.
Your diminishing spirit.
Look at the routes that others are taking;
their paths are far more attractive.
And inspiring. And faithful.
There is an easier road.

So what is to be done?

Make a choice to stay on the road
seen and unseen
onto which you have been called.
And if you find yourself in the company of one
you do not yet recognize
do not look down at the ground.
Look at him.
Look upon him.
And you may find yourself filled with light.

## PRAYER WORD

**this road, walk with me**

I am counted among those who go down to the Pit
Psalm 88.4

# [07] YOU ARE SO NAIVE

You always imagined yourself to be optimistic.
And took pride on being hopeful.
But now you understand.
You have been deluding yourself.
You are deeply pessimistic,
only surviving through occasional shots of wonder.
One single cynical action is enough to throw you
off balance.
How fragile is your hope.
You are so naive.


But as you spend time with this taunt
– and with the greater story –
allow your reasons for hope to rise once more to the surface.

Both the tradition and your own experience
may again reveal their gifts.
And you may rediscover that your hope is both
credible and full of possibility.

And your naivety may be revealed as the way into truth.
Only in this way, with open heart and open hands
may you be able to receive.


## PRAYER WORD

**open heart, open hands**

I am like those who have no help
Psalm 88.4

# [08] YOU DO NOT HAVE WHAT IT TAKES

You really do not.
You will fail.

And this is a repeating pattern.
Others have what it takes. But you don't.
You are weak.
You do not have what it takes.


But how true is this?
Sure, you don't have all it takes.
But you have a little of what is needed.
Just a drop perhaps, but sometimes a trickle, a stream,
in time a river – and sometimes a great surge
into an ocean of strength and will.
From where does this come?

Deep in your being there is an at-oneness with the divine
community who do have what it takes.

In the recognition that you lack everything
may come the understanding
that you lack nothing.


## PRAYER WORD

**I lack everything, I lack nothing**

I am like those forsaken among the dead
Psalm 88.5

# [09] YOU ARE THE KING, THE QUEEN OF THE WORLD

There are occasional moments when everything
goes your way. They make you feel invincible.
But most of the time you let others decide.

So often you act like a subject,
dependent on the whims or the decisions of others.
It's time to take some control.
To step into your power.
Do not let anyone else take responsibility for your happiness,
for your work, or for your legacy.
You are the king, the queen of the world!


There is some truth here.
You must live out your calling.
So give yourself to it with energy and with love.
But there's a question here around the use of power.
What kind of power do you wish to embody?

Find a different image.
One that reflects the possibilities of working
in collaboration with others,
in the mutual strength
of humility.


## PRAYER WORD

**in humility, strength**

I am like the slain that lie in the grave
Psalm 88.5

# [10] YOU ARE IN CONTROL OF NOTHING

You imagine that you can control your life.
You set out each day with a strong sense of where you are going
and of how you will get there.
But your day is thrown off balance
by the tone of a comment,
by a difficult conversation,
or by something in the news.
You are in control of nothing.

But the realization that you control nothing
– or very little – may be an uncomfortable gift.

What is your task?
It is not to control life
but to learn how to be in it,
to walk through it,
to engage with it
– with grace, with love, and with hope.

Don't try to control your life.
Rather, give attention to how you are within it,
each season,
each day,
each moment.
Today.

## PRAYER WORD

**today, grace**

I am like those whom you remember no more
Psalm 88.5

# [11] WORSHIP YOUR HURT

You have been hurt.
You have been abandoned,
ignored, belittled and betrayed.
Your hurt must be entered into.
Felt. Experienced.
Go deep into it.
Live from your hurt, find its energy.
It deserves your best – your worship.
And it will reward you.
Worship your hurt.


There is of course an element of truth here.
You need to recognize any hurt, to be real about it,
and to accept what has been done (or not done) to you.
But can you see how attractive it has become to you
to stir your hurt, to nurture it,
to make it the centre of your being –
to worship it?
This is so destructive.

Your hurt is just one element of the path you have taken
(or that has come your way unbidden).
It's time to remove your hurt from the centre of your being.
Time to take that bloody tin god off the table.
And to replace it
with an ikon of your love.


## PRAYER WORD

**from hurt, to love**

I am cut off from your hand
Psalm 88.5

# [12] TAKE SOMETHING FOR YOUR HURT

You feel the hurt.
It has a physical quality.
And it needs a physical remedy.

Take something for the hurt.
You know what you need.
Your go-to high.
Whatever gets you through the night.
Dull the pain, find your euphoria.
Take something for your hurt.

Euphoria is good.
A glimpse of your blissful at-oneness.
But is now the right time to go to it?
Find a way to live with the hurt first.
Or you may just be dealing with another symptom.

In God's grace there may be a way to hold the hurt,
and so in time to experience its transformation.

The healing you need for the hurt
is already waiting
within you.

## PRAYER WORD

**holding, transforming**

you have put me in the depths of the Pit

Psalm 88.6

# [13] YOU DO NOT BELONG HERE

You have always looked for somewhere to belong.
Somewhere to come home to.
But you do not belong here.
And you are not welcome.
Move on.
Leave this place.
You do not belong here.


The need to belong is part of your story.
But you are seeking to belong in a place that does not exist.
Doesn't everywhere offer both welcome and unease,
conveying both a hint of our settling
and a feeling of wilderness?

This wilderness journey is revealing that your true belonging
is within the life of God,
whose life is lived (amazingly, beautifully) also in you.

You have never been far from home.


## PRAYER WORD

**in you alone, I belong**

in the regions dark and deep
Psalm 88.6

# [14] YOU HAVE NOTHING TO SAY

Out here in the wilderness
the inadequacy of your words is revealed.
Kindling for a fire that never caught.
So much time spent on words.
But you have nothing to say.

And yet your experience of the inadequacy of your words
is in itself some small revelation.
At best they will only hint at what is true.
But when offered with authenticity and love
their poverty may reveal the abundance
of what it is they seek.

So give deep attention to your words.
Be alert for the spark that may light some new fire.
Then offer what comes into being,
words humbly seeking to resonate with the great Word.
And that offer will be enough.

For in allowing such a Word to take shape in *your* heart
at least one more human being
may find themselves
all flame.

## PRAYER WORD

**all flame**

your wrath lies heavy upon me
Psalm 88.7

# [15] YOU HAVE MADE YOUR OWN GOD

When you wake in the night
and sense your aloneness
does this not come as a dark revelation:
you have made your own God.
Building on the plans and construction sites of others
you have built your own deity.
You have made your own God.


The God you seek is the God you desire
The God you look for is the God you long for.
But is it possible that the God-who-truly-is
is inviting you to shape the God-presence where you are?

You, of course, cannot make God
anything other than God is.
You sense – you know intuitively –
what this God may be like.
And you trust what have been passed on as the greatest
revelations of the tradition.

In your experience and in the tradition, God is love.
Let *this* God shape the way you are.
Let this God make you.


## PRAYER WORD

**God is love**

and you overwhelm me with all your waves
Psalm 88.7

# [16] YOUR RELIGION BREAKS HERE

Your religion is a comfort.
A protective wall surrounding you.
Its rituals suggest strength.
But here and now, in this moment,
in this time of loss,
when disappointment bursts in your gut,
that strength is exposed.
It is just another idea.

And when the storm comes
your religion surely breaks, and you are shattered.
Your religion breaks here.


But perhaps a religion that breaks is a good religion.
A religion that exhibits no weakness is of little use.
The fragility of your religion is its strength,
calling you to construct nothing – in words or stone –
but to enter into its heart, and to live in its spirit.

Broken for you and for the world.
Welcome the breaking.


## PRAYER WORD

**breaking, welcome**

you have caused my companions to shun me
Psalm 88.8

# [17] YOUR GOD HEARS NOTHING

Your God is stone.
A pebble perhaps.
Beautiful but unhearing, unfeeling, and uncaring.
Your theology is geology.
The study of dead rocks.
You are not heard.
So stop speaking.
Your God hears nothing.


What if God hears,
but has little interest in your words –
or at least has less interest than you have in them?

What if this God is more interested
in your presence,
in your attention,
in your love?
Could your words be getting in the way?

Say what needs to be said,
then fall into silence.
Into presence.


## PRAYER WORD

**silence, presence**

you have made me a thing of horror to them
Psalm 88.8

# [18] THE ENDING IS INEVITABLE

You know how this will end.
In loss, fear, disappointment and darkness.
You seek out beauty.
You long to create magnificence.
But the ending will be neither beautiful nor magnificent.
It will be shambolic and painful.
The ending is inevitable.


Accept the inevitability of endings.
One of the great tasks of your life is to learn how to let go.
And to practise grace whenever endings come.

The dying away of a thing is rarely beautiful
but the trust that it can inspire
and the future that it ushers in
have their own beauty –
and may just be magnificent.

Great is the mystery of faith:
Christ has died.
Christ is risen.
Christ will come again.


## PRAYER WORD

**let go**

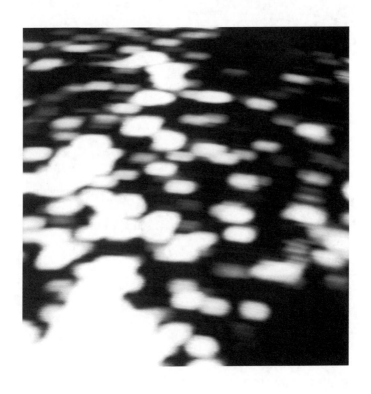

I am shut in so that I cannot escape
Psalm 88.8

# [19] STOP YOUR DREAMING

Your dreams once felt so real, so alive.
How hard now to see them smashed,
scattered remnants on the ground,
bleached bones.

You thought that life was for ever.
That your dreams of the better thing would always open up
in some beautiful future.
Now, the cold realization: your dreams are just dreams.
Slipping from your hands.
Dead.
Stop your dreaming.

Time to return to the valley.
To sit with the dry bones.
Let your imagination lift them gently from the dust.
And it may be that muscle, sinew and flesh
will begin to form around them.

Dream dreams, see visions.

## PRAYER WORD

**dream again**

my eye grows dim through sorrow
Psalm 88.9

# [20] YOU ARE TO BLAME

You are, of course, to blame.
It's your own stupid fault.
So much promise thrown away.
So many bad decisions.
How did you perfect that art?
Your hopes are in tatters.
You are to blame.


But all that you have done – and all that you have left undone
– have got you to this point.
They are your story.
You are to blame, yes.
And you are to take credit.
For the good things, for the good decisions,
for the sheer will to live each day in a demanding world.

Accept censure for what goes wrong.
Take the credit for what goes well.
And resolve to live without shame.


## PRAYER WORD

**no more shame**

every day I call on you, O Lord
Psalm 88.9

# [21] YOU ARE FORGOTTEN

You long to be remembered.
Not at some time in the future
(though that might be good).
But now.
To know that someone is thinking of you,
looking out for you, even longing for you.
But you are forgotten.


Is it possible that even this forgetting carries some dark gift?

Your sense of being forgotten is the necessary sifting process
by which you will come to realize that you have never been
separate, never alone, never just you.
Look around you.
Signs of your belonging, of your connection,
of your being remembered are all around.
Your sense of separation is an illusion.

Your self still matters.
But it is a self that is at the same time
both deeply individual,
and deeply at one with all, with God.

You are remembered.


## PRAYER WORD

**remembered**

I spread out my hands to you
Psalm 88.9

# [22] TAKE WHAT IS DUE TO YOU

For too long you have let others take the credit
for what you have done.
Now take what is due to you.
You have been too quiet.
Too meek.
You deserve accolades and success.
Take what is due to you.


It's true that you can be reticent in taking up
what may be offered to you.
But far more important to be true to who you are
and who you are called to be.
Let the outcome be what it will be.

You are not actually due anything.
That is the limiting world of reward and punishment,
of ownership and attachment.

Consider instead the flowers of the field,
lavished with love,
and seek to live as they live with grace, in grace, from grace.
And in this way you will receive
all that you need to thrive.


## PRAYER WORD

**as the flowers of the field**

do you work wonders for the dead?
Psalm 88.10

# [23] WHAT USE YOUR RITUALS HERE?

Do you really think that your rituals work?
They are just a flimsy fence in the path of a storm.
A comforting boundary marker on a sunny day perhaps,
but now about to be blown away.
No substance.
What use your rituals here?


But you sense a response to this taunt welling up within you,
deep in your spirit, in your thinking and in your body.
Your rituals point to a greater reality.

The storm is not the last word.
And your rituals are not a fence around you.
But the threshold onto some deeper truth
for which you are being shaped.
And the line between you and them is increasingly blurred.
The prayer, the stillness, the text, the bread and the wine.
They are part of you now.
Your rituals are markers of your true belonging.

God's holy gifts
for God's holy people.


## PRAYER WORD

**God's holy gifts**

do the shades rise up to praise you?
Psalm 88.10

# [24] HOW ARE YOU AT ALL SIGNIFICANT?

So, tell me exactly, how are you significant?
What are you doing that will in any way make a difference?
If you left the scene today, no one would notice.
And why should they?
How are you at all significant?

But within the truth of this taunt
there is a greater truth.
This humiliation opens up consolation.
Every small hopeful action you make today
– just another normal day –
is nurturing some ultimate good.
And who is to say that the small thing is less important
than some much honoured event?
You do not know the significance of what you do.
So don't try to justify it.

Simply do the small things, the hopeful things,
that you are called to do –
and become the person you are called to become.
And let any significance look after itself.

Seek the Way of the Beloved,
not the illusion of significance.

## PRAYER WORD

**the Way of the Beloved**

is your steadfast love declared in the grave?
Psalm 88.11

# [25] THE WORLD IS BROKEN

Totally broken. All around you.
The dehumanization of people in every possible way,
and destruction of our planet and of our fellow creatures.
And you are right to fear for your children
and for their children.
What are we leaving them?
You are broken.
Beyond repair.
The world is broken.


But the tradition has always recognized this challenge.
The prophets faced this.
Their faith produced the call into Tikkun Olam[2].
And our brokenness is only one strand
in the unfolding story.
The possibility of repair and healing is in your hands
(and in the hands of many other hopeful ones).

Resolve today to engage with others
in some small act of repair.
With faith, with hope, and with love.
Every day, your world is being repaired.


## PRAYER WORD

**remake, repair**

---

2 A Jewish concept that calls us to repair the world in our setting.

is your faithfulness declared in the place of destruction?
Psalm 88.11

# [26] NO ONE IS GOOD

There is no one good.
We are all barely holding it together.
Even the best is a clever surface act.
What lies beneath is a maelstrom of indifference,
bitterness and collusion.
Your belief that we are essentially good is falling apart.
Where's the evidence?
You are not good.
No one is good.


We are all trying to hold it together.
And often failing.
But look around and look within.
You know of your own yearning to be good
and to bring goodness to the world around you.
You are not alone in that desire.
People are good.
Many are extraordinarily so.
Sure, some have forgotten,
and some may never appear to recover their goodness.
But goodness is within you, and all around you.

Seek out goodness today. It is not far off.


## PRAYER WORD

**seeking goodness**

are your wonders known in the darkness?
Psalm 88.12

# [27] YOU CAN TRUST NO ONE

You have been shafted.
And the shafting will happen again.
They only want you for what you can bring to them.
Your trust is not reciprocated.
No one is trustworthy.
You can trust no one.


Sooner or later someone *will* let you down.
But does that really matter?
You can choose.
Most people most of the time are trustworthy.
And the more you trust people the happier you will be.
We respond to being trusted.
So trust someone today who you find difficult to trust.

And through it all the tradition is clear.
You can trust Some-One.


## PRAYER WORD

**I will trust**

is your saving help known in the land of forgetfulness?
Psalm 88.12

# [28] YOU WILL LET EVERYONE DOWN

You will let people down.
With or without intent.
Inevitably.
You always have.
And you always will.
You will let everyone down.


Some of the expectations placed upon you
are reasonable and right.
Do your very best to live up to these expectations.
And today is a new day.
Live it resolved not to betray these expectations.

But some of the hopes placed upon you are not reasonable;
they are more about those who are placing them
than about you.
Observe the difference.
Don't let these expectations affect you.

This is a new day.


## PRAYER WORD

**a new day**

but I, O Lord, cry out to you
Psalm 88.13

# [29] YOU ARE A HYPOCRITE

So convincing.
You may even convince yourself.
But you are a hypocrite.
Less of *this* than you claim to be.
More of *that* than you portray.

It's subtle, usually, of course,
but there's a difference between the show and the reality.
You allow reflections, deflections, and disturbances
on the surface to mask deeper realities.
You are a fraud.
You are a hypocrite.

But this is just part of the challenge of becoming
a good human being.

Give attention to becoming still,
as the settling of clouded water,
so that in stilled-transparency
the truth of whatever lies deep down may be revealed.

You need not be fearful of this disclosure.
Reveal who you are.

## PRAYER WORD

**becoming transparent**

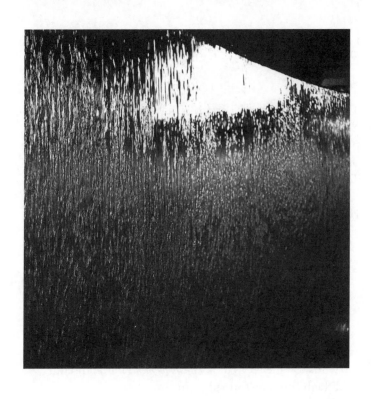

in the morning my prayer comes before you
Psalm 88.13

# [30] YOUR WORST MOMENTS ARE FOR EVER

They will always come back to disturb you.
You cannot just shake them off,
pretend that they didn't happen
or even declare that they are done with.
They will always define you.

Happy those who have never done anything underhand,
shameful or manipulative.
But you are not one of those.
Your worst moments are for ever.

Remember this.
In one of the key themes of the tradition
the Christ on the cross took *all our moments* into himself,
held them and transformed them.
Neither your worst – nor your best – moments are for ever.
All is transformed.
And all that will remain is love, the Lover and the Beloved.

Others may choose to define you as your worst
(or best) moments.
They have the right to do so.
But you, Beloved, have another choice.

## PRAYER WORD

**all is transformed**

O Lord, why do you cast me off?
Psalm 88.14

# [31] YOU DON'T REALLY BELIEVE ALL THAT DO YOU?

It offers some nostalgic comfort to you, of course.
And you have invested so much time into it over many years.
It has to matter to you.
To accept that you don't believe it would be embarrassing.
Shattering even.
But you don't really believe all that do you?


You could recall the names of all the wonderful people
who have inspired you who believe in the tradition.
And you could list the brilliant things
that have come into being through them.
Both worth doing perhaps.

But the most important thing is not any cerebral set
of beliefs you hold (as helpful as they can be).
But the way in which whatever you believe
may transform you for good.

Belief is stepping into a story that rings true
and allowing that story to form you.
The story must take shape again in you.
Any belief will find its believability in your life today.


## PRAYER WORD

**for good**

why do you hide your face from me?
Psalm 88.14

# [32] IT'S ALL ABOUT YOU

You put yourself at the centre of your everything.
The world spins around you.
Your thoughts, your feelings, your fears, your pleasures.
It's all about you.

Even your faith is about you.
Your journey, your reality, your life.
So much for being poor in spirit.
You think it's all about you.


But you do know that it's not all about you.
And gradually you are coming to realize
that it's about everything.
And about everyone.
And about our deep connection.
To the earth,
to each other,
and to the source of all being.

Look around you.


## PRAYER WORD

**all, one**

wretched and close to death from my youth up
Psalm 88.15

# [33] YOUR FUTURE IS IN YOUR HANDS

Do something and do it now.
The future is in your hands.
You can seize this moment.
No one else will do it for you.
It's all waiting for you.
Just throw yourself at it.
Reach out for it.
Your future is in your hands.


There is truth here of course.
You can make a difference.
And you may need to stop waiting for others
to decide the future for you.
Make good and bold choices now, today.

But have some humility.
Your future is, if you allow it to be so,
just one element in a greater future
that is already taking shape.
Nurture awareness of the deeper streams that
are at work,
and step into them.

You don't need to push this divine river.
The river flows, without end.


## PRAYER WORD

**river, flow**

I suffer your terrors
Psalm 88.15

# [34] MAKE YOURSELF COMFORTABLE

You are already good at doing this.
And so you should be.
It's what we've evolved to do.
It's how to survive.
Finding countless small ways to make ourselves comfortable.
And in a turbulent world surely it's not just natural
but important to do this.
What use are you in discomfort?
So make yourself comfortable.

Some comfort is not a bad thing, of course.
But this is about priority.

Your comfort alone is such an empty intention.
Give yourself rather to helping reshape the world for good.
And that task begins not in a search for comfort,
shielding yourself from the realities of existence,
but in a recovery of your sense of peace and belonging
*within and for* a frequently uncomfortable world.

In that quest the world will be healed
– and you will find the comfort you need.

## PRAYER WORD

**peace, healing**

I am desperate

Psalm 88.15

# [35] MAKE YOUR MARK ON THE WORLD

This world is passing you by.

You have gifts, passions and callings
that are going unseen.
They need to be lived and shared.
So make your mark, and make it now.
The blank canvas is waiting for you.
Make your mark on the world.


The world needs each of us to bring our goodness
and giftedness to it.
But it doesn't need your dominance, arrogance or greed.
Offer your mark, don't force it.
Share what you can with humility, generosity and joy.
Applaud the marks that others make in the same way.
The world is remade best when all bring their goodness to it.

And if your mark is rarely or never seen let this be.
Being-noticed is not part of the deal.
Just give what you are called to give,
offer what is springing up from within you.

The world does not need your mark.
It needs your love.


## PRAYER WORD

**my love**

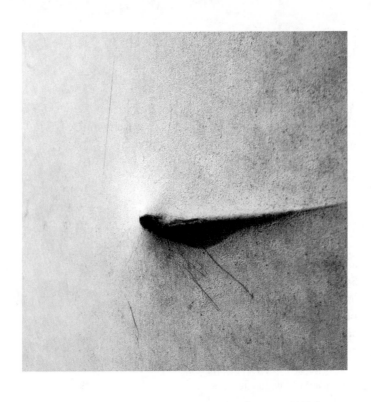

your wrath has swept over me
Psalm 88.16

# [36] YOU ARE NOT WORTHY

You are not worthy.
And you know you are not.
However you dress it up, however you present yourself,
you are so much less than you hoped to be,
imagined you would be, or could be.
You are not worthy.

Each Holy Week we come back to one of the great
and liberating themes of the faith.
Sure, you are not worthy,
in the sense of accumulated goodness,
but there is one who is,
and the Christ holds all your unworthiness
and transforms it.

You are worthy, his actions decide.
And yet even deeper than that,
if you recognize yourself
as another sketch-in-progress of the heavenly things
and as ever more at one with God,
you will realize that it's not about worthiness.
It's about something else.

You are loved.

## PRAYER WORD

**loved**

your dread assaults destroy me
Psalm 88.16

# [37] ALL LIGHT WILL FADE

What seems dark now is nothing
compared to the darkness that is coming.
You are in half light now.
Even that will be extinguished.
All light will fade.


But isn't every night and day an experience
of light's fading and returning?
And perhaps a taste of greater patterns at work.
The fading light that you fear
brings with it the hope of light returning,
light from dark.

In this Holy Week may you have the courage to enter fully
into the darkness of Good Friday,
and the despair of Holy Saturday,
and to wait for whatever may come,
knowing that you are not alone.

But first comes the fading of the light, as it must.


## PRAYER WORD

**with me, in the fading light**

they surround me like a flood all day long
Psalm 88.17

# [38] THE WILD ANIMALS WILL KILL YOU

They surround you.
They wait.
Your fears encircle you.
And they will devour you.
The wild animals will kill you.


This taunt calls for courage.
To look the wild animals in the eye.
To return their hostile gaze
with a gaze of a very different kind.

They may kill you in the end.
But they cannot kill your spirit.
Or the source of your hope.
Or your love.


## PRAYER WORD

**return the gaze**

from all sides they close in on me
Psalm 88.17

# [39] STOP THIS NOW, WALK AWAY

Everything is in the balance.
Your hope.
Your faith.
Your existence.
You do not have to remain on this path.
Stop this now, walk away.


Except you know that you *must* carry on.
And what pulls you on is not duty, or fear,
but love.

You realize now that
the paths of love and suffering
are inextricably linked.

May you be blessed with the courage to take the next step
towards the love that you seek.


## PRAYER WORD

**towards the love**

you have caused friend and neighbour to shun me
Psalm 88.18

# [40] SO WHERE ARE THE ANGELS?

You've followed the wilderness path for 40 days.
Now you are in a very dark place.
All those warnings ignored, you persisted.
And here you are,
in darkness,
on the ground,
forgotten,
unheard,
lost.

Did you really think they would come?
With great wings
shimmering with light,
to lift you up?
So, where are the angels?


For now, you must wait in this tomb.
Give yourself only to love.
Love, even now, for the memory of God,
love for the memory of each neighbour.
And remember the love shown to you.

That love, all these loves, they persist.
Only love will remain.


## PRAYER WORD

**only love**

my companions are in darkness
Psalm 88.18

# IDEAS FOR REFLECTION AND ACTION

## WORKING WITH THE PRAYER WORD

In the wilderness Jesus responded to the tempter's taunts with short phrases of Scripture. The Prayer Words here are offered from my own wilderness experience.

1  Allow the Prayer Word to settle quietly within you in time and balance with your breathing, perhaps the first word(s) on the in-breath, the remaining word(s) on the out-breath. Try a brief pause before each in-breath and each out-breath.

2  Let this repeated Prayer Word carry all your yearnings, becoming both your prayer and your resolution.

3  Whenever you recognize your attention wandering (as it will) return to your Prayer Word.

4  If you ever find yourself able to let go of the Prayer Word and simply be fully present in the moment, enjoy the possibility of divine encounter.

## WORKING WITH LECTIO DIVINA

1  Read a passage from one of the Gospel narratives of the temptation of Jesus.

2  What catches your attention?

3  How might the word or phrase that has caught your attention be a gift to you at this time?

4  Pray with the phrase that has caught your attention, allowing it to carry all your hopes and prayers.

5  Let the phrase fall away – enter stillness.

PRAYER WORD
becoming both your prayer and your resolution

## WORKING WITH THE 40 TAUNTS

1 Read one of the 40 Taunts.

2 What (if anything) in this taunt resonates with your own experience?

3 What alternative or additional taunts might be thrown at you at this time?

4 Did Jesus face a similar taunt – and, if so, how did he appear to handle it?

## WORKING WITH THE IMAGES

1 Give your attention to an image. What feelings does it produce in you?

2 Be curious about light and shade in the image.

3 If you take photographs, take some photos that reflect the sombre beauty – the wilderness – of your own environment.

## MAKING ART

1 Take one of the temptations faced by Jesus – or a line from Psalm 88 – and in response create a piece of art in your chosen field (painting, music, photography, poem, prose, drama etc.).

2 You could set the piece in your own current context.

3 In a group setting you could invite each person to choose a different phrase from the Gospel narrative, or from Psalm 88 or one of the Taunts as inspiration for a piece of work, and then gather the works together for a conversation (or even an exhibition). Conversation about the creative process invariably opens up new learning and possibilities.

the possibility of divine encounter